HELPING YOU WIN WITH MONEY ONE DAY AT A TIME

simple financial concepts

How to Take Back

Control of Your Money

Shane Lundbohm

© 2018 by Shane Lundbohm
All rights reserved. No portion of this book may be reproduced in any form or by any means without the prior written permission of the publisher.

This book is sold with the understanding that the author and publisher are not engaged in rendering financial, accounting, or other professional advice. Each individual situation is unique and if financial advice or other expert assistance is required, the services of a competent professional should be sought. The author and publisher disclaim any liability, loss, or risk resulting directly or indirectly, from the use or application of any of the contents of this book.

ISBN 9781719225113

TABLE OF CONTENTS

Introduction   5

  1. Budgeting   15
    How to Do One and Why It's So Important

  2. Debt   29
    Go Against the Norm

  3. Saving   43
    Rainy Days Will Come…Be Prepared!

  4. Spending   53
    Homes, Cars & Other Major Purchases

  5. Retirement   63
    How to Make Sure the Golden Years Stay Golden

  6. Kids, College & Prioritizing   79
    A.K.A. How to NOT Wreck Your Retirement Plans

  7. Insurance   91
    What You Need and What You Don't

  8. Giving   101
    Because It's Not All About You

  9. Your Action Plan   109

INTRODUCTION

My Story & Why I Wrote This Book

All of my life I've compared myself to others. I still catch myself doing it to this day even though I know better. It could be someone in a brand new Mercedes stopped next to me at a stoplight or a person with the new iPhone. Heck, I've even gotten jealous of fictional characters on TV shows when they're dressed up all fancy on their way to an event. Don't tell me you haven't done it (okay, maybe that last one is just me). The point is that I have a bit of a contentment problem.

I was born and raised in Tucson, Arizona for the first 12 years of my life. My family lived in a trailer park in a rough area of town, but it was never really an issue for me. My two sisters and I always had what we needed and much of our childhood was spent as a family sightseeing the natural beauty of Arizona. One thing my parents were always good at was finding fun things to do that didn't cost a lot of money. My father was a mechanical engineer and one summer he used leftover scrap metal from work to make side skirts for our trailer. He and I worked on it together and it turned out really nice. We definitely had the best looking lot in the trailer park (although there wasn't much competition)!

When I was 12 years old, we moved to Auburn, Alabama, and as a pre-teen I started noticing things relating to class divide. The popular kids at school had nicer clothes and cool gadgets, and suffice it to say, I was not one of the popular kids. My parents didn't see the point in wasting money on stuff like that when we were perfectly fine with what we had. There were moments when they definitely tried to understand how I felt, however. One year, I remember for months I was begging my parents to get me an Auburn Tigers jacket because all of the cool kids had one. Just when I had given up all hope, on Christmas morning I opened up one of my presents and there it was: a navy blue and orange Auburn Tigers jacket. I was so elated and wore it everywhere.

We moved to Maryland, just outside Washington, D.C., before my sophomore year in high school. That was when I really started feeling the effects of not being one of the "haves." Don't get me wrong, I still had everything I needed to get by, but by that point it was clear to me that we were not and probably never would be upper class. There was also a bit of culture shock. In Arizona, the far majority of people were very laid-back and comparison never seemed to be an issue. When I lived in Alabama, there was a little bit of it, but not nearly as much as in Maryland. Being in the Washington, D.C. area, it was amplified to an extreme degree with everyone constantly trying to outdo each other in their displays of wealth.

All of this competition and degree of wealth (later I would learn, a lot of it wasn't really wealth) led me down a road of poor financial decision-making which started around the age of 18 and lasted all throughout my twenties. I signed up for my first credit card not long after turning 18 and quickly got two more after that. The notion that I would have to pay back any money that I charged didn't really register with me at the time, and I maxed out all three cards. Actually, I went over the limit on them and accrued penalty fees monthly. My father ended up helping me out by paying to get me back under the limit (even though he couldn't really afford it).

At 19, I was working full-time as a new car salesman at a Toyota dealership. Even though I was a horrible salesman (I think I may have sold three cars in the six months I had that job), I had the bright idea that I should purchase a new 2000 Toyota Celica GT on a five-year loan at 19% interest, giving me monthly payments of $471. Meanwhile, I was living at home and making minimum wage. The only decision I made that worked in my interest in that deal was buying gap insurance, which came in handy a year and a half later when I fell asleep while delivering newspapers in the middle of the night and hit a parked car head-on, totaling the Celica.

To top it off, throughout my twenties, I was attending college off and on, but paying for it all with student loans because you can't really pay for college when you only make minimum wage. I changed majors four times and in the end, didn't even finish my degree.

By the time I turned thirty, I was getting sick and tired of the whole comparison game and buying things that I really couldn't afford to impress friends and strangers. I started seeing friends get married and buy houses, and it hit me. Enough was enough. If I ever wanted to get any traction in my finances, I had to stop playing this game.

Over the next several years, I spent most of my free time learning all I could about personal finance. The funny thing is it's really not that hard. It takes discipline, yes (which is hard), but the principles are simple.

If I had a dollar for every regret I've had in my life, I'd be a very wealthy man. If Doc Brown showed up in his DeLorean and offered to take me back to my teenage years, I'd have a whole list of things I would do differently. The truth is that we all have things in our lives that we wish we could do over. Ask that girl out before someone else does. Study a little harder for that test to get an A instead of a C. Not buy that $50,000 SUV when we really don't need it. For me, my biggest regrets are the financial decisions that I made in my twenties. Had I only known at the time what I know now, I would have done a lot of things differently.

We all have baggage. The good news is that we can choose not to continue carrying it. When I said at the age of thirty that enough was enough, I made the decision to live a different life. I wasn't going to keep making stupid financial decisions to try to keep up with the Joneses. The days of going to Target and aimlessly pushing a cart down the aisles just looking for things to buy were over. I decided to live with purpose, and in the process I discovered a few things about myself. The first one was that I am a spender. I'm the type of person that if I have twenty dollars in my wallet, I'm going to find something to buy no matter how dumb it is. I also learned that I have a real problem with comparison. I couldn't stand to see a friend or a co-worker doing better than me (even if it was just the appearance of doing better) by driving a nicer car or getting the new iPhone or taking a vacation to Florida. I just had to keep up! I became a born-again Christian around the same time that I started my financial re-discovery, which helped a lot with dealing with my contentment problems, but boy, did I have a way to go!

A third thing I discovered about myself is that I have a really hard time saying no to people. I have a family member who was constantly in financial trouble because of poor choices (worse than mine), and developed a habit of coming to me for money. Well, I developed a habit of giving her money just about every time she asked because I couldn't stand the thought of what would happen if I said no. Would she hate me? Would she be out on the street? I was so worried about how my saying no would impact her that I had become a doormat and an enabler. She kept coming to me for money because she knew I would say yes! Eventually, after a few years of doing this, I knew it had to stop. It wasn't helping her any, plus it was costing me a fortune. The next time she asked for money, I put my foot down and said no (and in the process pretty much told her exactly what I thought about her bad habits in a not-so-nice manner). Feelings were hurt and we didn't talk for a year or so, but eventually we developed a healthier relationship with boundaries in place.

Many of you know exactly what I'm talking about. Whether it's relational, financial, or maybe even an unhealthy relationship with food, we all have baggage.

Today, I want to invite you to leave your baggage behind you. You can make better financial decisions—you just may not know how to yet. That's where I'm going to help you in this book. If you're like I was ten years ago, you may have never done a budget and the thought of it is overwhelming. Maybe you are up to your ears in credit card debt and just want to never see that statement in your mailbox again. Some of you may have never had a savings account and think that you never will because you'll never have anything to put in it. Perhaps you're getting a strong desire to buy a house, but don't even know where to begin.

    It's hard to sort through all the things that are being thrown at us on the news, in social media, and from our friends and family that sometimes it can just be overwhelming. We're being pulled in several different directions at all times, it seems, and a lot of the things we hear conflict with each other. You may have a friend telling you to use your credit card for everything because you'll get rewards points (bad idea). Whole-life insurance agents are saying that their products are great investments (a lie). Your well-meaning cousin says that you should hurry up and buy a house now before interest rates go up, even though you only have enough for a 3% down payment (don't do it!).

Over the course of this book, I will lay out the principles that I have learned and show you how to start winning with your money. Sit back and get ready for the ride!

1

BUDGETING

How to Do One & Why It's So Important

Budgeting can be very overwhelming if you've never done it and don't know where to start. *"I'm not an accountant. I can't do a budget."* Thoughts like this may have run through your mind. The good news is that it's not nearly as hard as you think it is to get started. The bad news is that it's going to take a few months to work out all the kinks and get your budget to be effective. Having patience will pay off, however, so don't despair!

Before I get into the basics of budgeting, I want to explain the importance of it and why you need one. I have a good friend who we'll call Seth that makes a pretty good income of over $120,000 per year. Seth owns a newer home in northern Virginia, drives a $55,000 Mercedes-Benz, and regularly goes on vacations to Europe and Hawaii. He also is one of the first ones to get a new iPhone when it is released and enjoys treating himself to massages on a regular basis.

Seth and I were having a conversation a few weeks ago where he laid this out for me and then followed with, "I have an enjoyable life and make a good income, but I'm still living paycheck to paycheck. I thought once I had a six-figure income, all of my financial problems would go away."

I asked Seth if he lived on a budget each month, and he looked at me funny and said, "Budget? I make six figures, why would I need to do that?" I began to see what the root of Seth's financial struggles was, and also a common misconception, which is that if you have a lot of money coming in, budgets become unnecessary. That couldn't be further from the truth and I would even argue that they're more necessary if you have a large income because you're more apt to waste your money on frivolous things.

Doing a budget helps you aim at your goals and achieve your dreams. Have you been dreaming of taking a trip to Italy to taste the wonderful food and see the beautiful sights? Budgeting can help you get there and give you a sense of when it might be feasible to take that trip. Are you tired of driving a car that breaks down every other week and desperately want to buy a new one? If you plan for it in the budget, you'll know when you can buy a new one. On the other hand, if you don't make a plan for your money, it will disappear. Believe me, I spent over a decade wondering where my money went and it was usually somewhere I didn't want it to go. Maybe that's you as well. Have you spent countless Thursdays with no money to spend, just waiting for Friday to come so your bank account is replenished? I have, and it's not fun.

Budgeting is also a biblical action. In Luke 14:28-30, Jesus tells his disciples, "For which of you, desiring to build a tower, does not first sit down and count the cost, whether he has enough to complete it? Otherwise when he has laid a foundation and is not able to finish, all who see it begin to mock him, saying 'This man began to build and was not able to finish.' "

Not many of us are building towers nowadays, but we can relate. I have a friend who owns a beach house in Virginia and I've been invited down many times over the years. On the way, I drive by a house that is in the middle of renovation and has been for as long as I can remember. It has no siding, just the plastic sheet wrap that you put up beforehand. Obviously, at some point these people were planning on redoing the siding on their house but something happened and they couldn't finish. Maybe these people are embarrassed by that, maybe they're not. I don't know them so I couldn't tell you. All I know is that they live in a house covered in plastic wrap.

On the other end of the spectrum, let's say you get a huge tax refund at the end of the year. If you're not living on a budget, that money will be gone before you know it and chances are, you'll have no idea where it went. I've made this mistake many times. The refund check would come and I'd immediately go to the mall and act like I just won the lottery. If you're budgeting and you make a plan for that money, you could pay down debt, save it to go toward a car replacement or even take a nice vacation (assuming you plan for it).

Warnings

Before we start, I want to forewarn you: your budget will not be perfect the first month. It may not even work at all. This is because we're human and we forget things, such as school field trips or birthday presents. Some of the initial numbers may be totally unrealistic, like what you plan to spend on groceries or entertainment. To combat some of these issues, I suggest you take out your previous month's bank statement and go through it with a fine-tooth comb. What did you spend at the grocery store? Are there any abnormalities that you see that don't occur every month? It's not going to fix everything, but it will help you make your budget more realistic.

After the first month, you're going to be tempted to give up. You will feel like it's hopeless and that life just throws way too many unexpected things at you to even consider living on a budget. DON'T GIVE UP! It will get better as you continue doing it. The second month will be better than the first, and the third month better than the second. After three months of doing your budget, you will be able to anticipate things that you hadn't thought of in the past.

If you're single, the good news is that you can make all of your budgeting decisions by yourself. You won't have a spouse to run things by and make compromises with. The bad news is that you won't have any accountability when you start to get off track, and you WILL get off track. As a single guy, this is a major struggle for me even to this day. I'll go to Target or Wal-Mart and see something I want to buy that isn't in the budget and I'll start trying to justify making the purchase. *Oh, it's only $20. I can just take it out of next week's spending money.* The problem is that if you keep borrowing from next week, it's not much better than living on a credit card. That's why it's essential for singles to have a trusted friend or family member serve as an accountability partner. You need someone to bounce thoughts off of, especially when you're about to make a major purchase such as a car, a house, or even a new television. Find someone who you already believe to be wise and makes good financial decisions themselves, and ask if he or she would be willing to be that person you go to when you need an opinion about a major financial decision. Chances are, they'll be flattered that you asked and more than happy to help.

If you're married, the good news is that you have built-in accountability. If you're about to buy (or do) something stupid, your spouse will let you know! For budgeting together, it is essential that you are on the same page. That is where having a monthly meeting comes into play. Schedule an hour with your spouse at the end of each month where the two of you will sit down and plan your budget for the next month together. If you have kids, make sure they are occupied with something while you are having the meeting so that you aren't interrupted.

One warning about doing a budget together with your spouse—chances are that you are going to get into an argument. In most marriages, one person is a spender and the other is a saver. Naturally, you're going to butt heads while doing the budget. When one of you wants to eat out every other night and the other wants to put a third of your income into a savings account, that's going to cause an argument. You're going to have to compromise, and if you've never done a budget before, that's difficult at first.

Remember the goal though: you both want to win with money, so you need to develop a plan that works for BOTH of you. The bottom line is that it's YOUR budget. If you want your eating out category to be $500 a month and you can afford it, there's nothing wrong with that. Just make sure you're in agreement about it. Money fights and problems are the number one cause of divorce in America today, so budgeting together is a great contributor to a healthy marriage.

The first time you do a budget, you may be in for a shock as to how much you spend on certain things. For me, it was the amount I spent on eating out. The first time I did a budget and looked at my bank statement from the previous month, I discovered I had spent over $400 getting take-out! I knew I was eating out a lot but I had no idea I was spending that much! Let's just say the next month was much different.

How to Do a Budget

Let's get down to the details of budgeting. Before worrying about categories like take-out, entertainment, or vacations, we want to take care of the essentials:

- **Housing & basic utilities**
- **Food (Groceries)**
- **Basic clothing**
- **Transportation**

If you have money for those four things, you can get by, and then you can start planning for additional items. If you work on commission and have a month where your income is very low, these are the categories you want to budget for first, *no matter what.* Never pay a credit card collector before you pay these things. Your family is more important than your credit score, and taking care of the basics comes first. I will go into more detail about this later.

The best way to budget is the zero-based plan. Don't worry; it's nothing fancy and very easy to do. What this means is that you are going to give all of your money for the month a plan so that your income minus your expenses equal zero.

TOTAL INCOME – TOTAL EXPENSES = 0

Write your total income at the top of the page and then write all of your expenses for that month underneath it. Make sure you include EVERYTHING and that means any giving and saving amounts as well. Everything that you list in your expense column should add up *exactly* to the amount you wrote at the top under income. If it doesn't, you'll need to go back and make some adjustments so that it does. Take a look at this sample budget so you can see what I mean:

TOTAL INCOME (net)	$3,500
Rent	$850
Utilities	$250
Groceries	$200
Car insurance	$50
Gas	$80
Giving	$350
Netflix	$10
Eating out	$80
Savings (retirement)	$525
Savings (house down pmt)	$1,105
TOTAL EXPENSES	**$3,500**

Once you have your preliminary budget complete, think and make sure you didn't leave anything out. Do you have any doctor appointments coming up that require a co-pay? Is a friend or family member having a birthday that you'll need to buy a gift for? Think hard, and you'll lessen the chance of having to panic mid-month when you realize you forgot something.

If you have money left over after writing down your expenses and wondering what to do with it, my first suggestion would be to make sure you have $1,000 set aside in a savings account for minor emergencies. That way you won't have to use a credit card the next time the car breaks down. You'll be able to just pay for it, and there's no stress about when you'll be able to pay that credit card off.

If you're in the opposite situation and you find that you have more money going out than coming in, you're going to have to make some decisions as to how to get those income and expense numbers to match up. Obviously we can't spend more money than we make, so something will need to be reduced or cut. Discuss possibilities with your spouse (if you're married). Maybe you can lower your entertainment budget, or pack lunches for the kids so they don't need to buy it. It's your budget, so it's up to you.

Helpful Tips

Doing the budget is great, but don't forget that you actually have to live on it. This was my problem at first. I would make myself a great-looking budget and got it down to a science, but then I would deviate from it throughout the month by overspending on food or entertainment. That pretty much made doing a budget pointless, so I had to start having some discipline. Personal finance is 80% behavior and only 20% head knowledge. You can have all the smarts in the world but if you don't apply it, *it's worthless*.

For some categories (especially the ones that you know you will be tempted to overspend on), an excellent way to succeed in sticking to the budget is to take cash out at the ATM and either clip it together or put it in an envelope, labeling what it is for. When McDonald's started accepting credit cards several years back, *their average sale jumped 47%*. This is because when swiping a card, you don't feel the money leaving like you do when you're handing over cash. Cash gets more of an emotional reaction from people. If you allocate $30 to your weekly "blow" money, take $30 out of the bank and stick it in an envelope. When the envelope is empty, you're out of money!

If you're someone who has an irregular income (you have a sales or commission-based job), that doesn't give you a pass on budgeting. It just means you'll have to do it slightly differently. You're going to make a list of your spending priorities each month from most important to least important, and allocate your income in that order. If you have a great month of income, you might get to do everything on the list. If you have a slow month, you may only be able to do half the list. Just remember to cover your first four basic categories first (food, housing, clothing and transportation).

In the back of this book, there is a sample budgeting form that you can use to get started. Remember, *make it your own*. The categories I have listed are just to get you started. You may have more or fewer categories than what I have listed and that's okay!

2

DEBT

Go Against the Norm

When I was 19 years old, I was working full-time as a new car salesman at a Toyota dealership. That alone should have been a warning sign that I was headed down the wrong path because I'm as introverted as they come and approaching random people to try and sell them a new car was not a strength of mine. Regardless, a few months into that job, I decided I needed a new car. *I'm an adult now and adults buy new cars and I work full-time, so this is what I'm supposed to do.* That's what I told myself anyway.

I picked out a white 2000 Toyota Celica GT from the lot that I thought looked cool, glanced at the sticker price of slightly over $20,000, and didn't think too much of it. *That's what loans are for.* I went over to the finance office where one of my colleagues I was friendly with drew up the papers for me. I looked at my monthly payment and briefly thought to myself, wait, that's about as much as I make in one paycheck, but then quickly tried to rationalize it by telling myself that I'm just going to have to start selling more cars (like it was that easy).

For the next year-and-a-half, I forked over almost $500 a month so I could drive my nice, brand new, sporty car around town and look cool. I couldn't afford to do much of anything once I got to my destination, but at least I looked good getting there!

Debt is Normal

Having debt is normal in America. As I write this, the national debt is over 20 TRILLION DOLLARS. We, as a culture, are very good at borrowing money. According to CreditCards.com, 167 million Americans have at least one credit card. That's 72% of us that are going to the store and swiping a card, just hoping that we'll be able to pay it back when the bill comes. It's gotten to the point where if you don't own a credit card, you're considered weird. I haven't had a credit card in several years now, and I often get strange looks when I tell people that.

What about student loans, which are now the second biggest debt category that we have as a country? We encourage our kids to go to college, which is great, but most of us never stop and think about how to pay for it. With the cost of college tuition rising every year, this is becoming a bigger and bigger problem. According to the College Board, annual tuition at a 4-year state college during the 2016-17 school year averaged $9,650. At first glance, that doesn't seem that bad, but that's only one category. Do you have a child that wants to go to school out of state? That's going to run you an average of $24,930 per year. What if you have a kid that wants to go to a private college? **$33,480 per year is the average cost.** That's insane! What's even more insane, however, is the number of people who just get a loan for that amount even though there is no guarantee that they will get a high or even decent paying job after they graduate. According to a study done by the Federal Reserve

Bank of New York, 62% of recent college graduates are working in a job that doesn't even require a degree! Only they're dragging around with them a huge amount of student loan debt that's going to take them decades to pay off.

    I fell victim to this trap myself. After high school, I had absolutely no idea what I wanted to do with my life, so I did what I thought was expected of me and signed up for classes at the local community college. I looked at the list of majors and settled on computer science because I heard that you could make decent money at it. Never mind that I knew nothing about computers aside from Microsoft Word and Excel and surfing the internet, nor was I all that interested in them. Well, my first college experience lasted all of a semester because I failed all of my classes. I wasn't ready for college and didn't have a real reason for being there, so half the time I didn't go to class or give any real effort at all. My parents found out about it, and since they were the ones who were financing my education, they informed me that they would be doing so no longer.

The History of Debt in America

Believe it or not, debt has not always been such an ingrained part of American culture. It wasn't until the 1980s that the concept blew up and everyone and their brother started borrowing for everything. In 1970, for example, only 15% of Americans had a credit card. A lot of major retailers were against the concepts of debt and credit and didn't even accept them in their stores.

Take J.C. Penney, for example. Do you know what the "C" stands for? Cash. James "Cash" Penney hated credit so badly that he didn't allow it in his stores while he was alive. Henry Ford was another person that didn't believe in debt. General Motors and Chrysler Corporation were in the business of making auto loans for ten years before Ford started doing it. Nowadays, large companies like these make more money off of loan interest than they do by selling their products!

On a more personal level, ask your grandparents or even your parents how debt played a role in their lives when they were younger. Chances are that it played little to no role at all. If they wanted something, they had to save up the money to buy it.

Is it possible to live without debt? Absolutely. Let's take a look at some myths surrounding it.

Myths about Debt

"I can't go to college without student loans."

Actually, there are several ways you can go to college without borrowing money. For starters, there are tons of scholarship opportunities available that most people overlook. Start by going to your counselor's office if you're in high school or the financial aid office if you're already in college. They have lists of scholarship resources for you. In addition to that, a quick Google search will give you a bunch of websites that can help.

In addition to scholarships, there are grants available from the federal government and also the state you live in. Grants are basically free money for college that do not have to be repaid (except in rare circumstances). Most students qualify for some kind of grant, so it's definitely worth checking out. See the federal student aid website or your state's website for details.

A third way to go to college without borrowing money is to work. Yes, work your way through school! I know someone who did this and graduated in four years with zero debt, so it can definitely be done. You will need to find a job that pays more than minimum wage, but that can easily be done with a little searching. There has also been a growing trend of college students starting their own small business, which can often pay a lot more than working for someone else!

One more way to go to school without loans is to simply go to a cheaper school. Don't think that you need an Ivy League education to get a good job. You don't. There is nothing wrong with state schools or community colleges. Some of them are very highly rated and most give great educations. Between scholarships, grants, and working hard while you're in school, you can easily graduate debt-free.

"Aren't there some good debts?"

Usually when people ask this question, they're concerned about maintaining their credit score. Americans as a whole are obsessed with credit scores and people have the idea that if you have a high score then you're some kind of whiz with money. Unfortunately, that is a lie that has been fed to consumers by banks and lending institutions.

If you have a high credit score, all that means is that you're good at managing debt. It doesn't mean that you're wealthy, financially successful, or even smart with money. You just know how to play the game that the bank wants you to play. There are many, many people out there that will claim that living without debt or a credit score is impractical. A lot of them are financial advisors and economists. Just because they say it, however, doesn't mean it's true. Is it more inconvenient? Sometimes, but it's worth the peace of mind.

So no, there is no such thing as a good debt. The only debt I like is one that is paid off.

"Having a car payment is not a big deal."

Really? The average car payment in America as of this writing is $503 per month, according to Experian. That's a lot of money to be spending on something that is going down in value each month. When I was younger, I used to think that it was a big deal to have a new car. I could impress my friends and random people at stoplights and pretend I was important. Looking back on that now, I think about how much money I wasted in the process.

The truth is, if you spend your life making car payments, there is a very good chance that you will never be wealthy. The average millionaire drives a two or three-year old car that they bought used and paid cash for, which is a habit formed before becoming wealthy. Money wasn't wasted on monthly car payments, but saved up and used to pay cash for reasonable cars.

"I don't need an emergency fund because I can just use my credit card or get a loan in the case of an emergency."

The absolute worst time to go into debt is when you have an emergency. Emotions are already running high and debt is going to send you into full-drama mode. Think about it; let's say your car dies unexpectedly and you quickly need to get a new one so you can go to work. If you have an emergency fund saved up with five to ten thousand dollars in it, you'll be able to just take out a portion of that and buy a slightly used car. If you're broke, what are you going to do? You'll go down to the dealer and sign a loan for a more expensive car than you would have bought with cash, and then finance it over five or six years. You let something that could have just been a minor inconvenience turn into a huge financial commitment!

Lending Money

On the other end of the spectrum from going into debt is helping someone else do so. I'm talking about lending money to people, and it's a really bad idea. There's an old joke that goes, "If you lend your brother-in-law a hundred dollars and he never talks to you again, was it worth the investment?" We laugh, but lending money to family or friends is a good way to ruin relationships.

I learned this lesson the hard way. Once I got out of debt and started having some extra money, one of my family members asked me for a loan. I was hesitant at first, as I knew it was a bad idea but I started feeling bad and relented, loaning her $1,000. She promised to pay me back within two months and I believed her even though I had my doubts. Two months went by, then a third and fourth month and I had yet to see a dime. I started getting angry every time I saw her and in my head began questioning every financial decision she made while she wasn't paying me back. Eventually, I did get the majority of the money back but it was not pleasant and feelings were hurt.

If you can afford to help out a friend or family member, it's best to just give them the money with no strings attached (assuming you agree with what it's going to be used for—you don't want to go around handing out money to alcoholics or drug addicts, as that would be enabling). Be sure to make it crystal clear to the person that the money is a one-time gift and that you're expecting them to be responsible with it. That's not being a control freak—it's good stewardship.

Bible Matters

As a Christian, I make it a habit of looking to the Bible for wisdom on a lot of things in life, but particularly financial matters since it's a passion of mine. The Bible has quite a few things to say about debt. Proverbs 22:7 says it clear as day: "The borrower is slave to the lender." SLAVE. I don't like that word, and I don't want to be a slave to anyone. When you borrow money, however, that's how it can feel. Sending loan payments to the bank every month to pay for something that seems like it's yours but isn't really until it's paid off makes the bank in charge of you.

Let me be clear, using debt is not a sin or a salvation issue, but the Bible makes it very clear that it is unwise. Take a step back before you think you "need" to use debt and consider other options.

The Best Way to Get Out of Debt

If you're in debt and ready to get out and stay out, the best and most effective method to use is the debt snowball. In this method, you will list your debts in order from smallest to largest balance. Note that I said balance, not interest rate. You want to ignore the interest rates for now. *But Shane, that doesn't make sense mathematically. If I paid my debts off according to interest rate, it would go quicker.* No, actually, it probably wouldn't. You're about to embark on a major life change by getting and staying out of debt, and what do we all know about making huge changes in our lives? IT'S HARD! Changes are hard to stick to because we naturally want to do what feels comfortable and easy.

The goal of using this method to pay off our debts is to get some quick wins. It's easier to pay off small credit card bills than it is to pay off an auto loan with a $20,000 balance. When you send that last payment to the credit card in a couple months (rather than the year or so that it may take to pay off the auto loan), you're going to feel accomplished. It's going to hit you—*Hey, I'm not going to see that bill anymore!* You'll start to get the sense that your hard work is starting to pay off and you're more likely to keep going!

If you're paying off your debt in the order of interest rate, the debt with the lowest interest rate could be the one with the highest balance. If that's the first bill you're starting with, it's going to seem daunting and when you go month after month and don't see much movement, chances are you're going to give up and return to a life of making monthly payments because it's easier and that's just the way people live. You'll feel a sense of hopelessness, and I don't want that for you. Try it my way. I guarantee it will work if you put in the effort.

Once you start down the path of getting out of debt, you have to make sure you're very intentional about it. You should already be living on a written budget, as I talked about in the previous chapter, but make sure you are *sticking* to the budget. It's one thing to make a budget, but a whole other thing to actually live on it. You have to be able to say no to other people and most importantly, to yourself. *No, I can't go out to eat tonight. No, you can't play 5 different sports this school year. No, we're not going to Disney World this year.* We're on a mission! We are getting out of debt and we are doing it quickly! The more intense and purposeful you are about attacking your debt, the quicker you will be able to put it in your past.

Once You Are Out of Debt

I will go deeper into detail in this in the next chapter but once you are out of debt, what's going to stop you from going back into it the next time something comes up? The answer: MONEY. You need to build up an emergency fund so that you're prepared the next time the roof has a leak or your car breaks down. Cut up the credit cards once and for all and live on cash. It's what wealthy people do to become wealthy, and if they did it, so can you.

3

SAVING

Rainy Days Will Come...Be Prepared!

Saving money has always been a bit of a challenge for me. I'm someone that would be considered a natural spender, and have been for as long as I can remember. To this day, if I find myself with an extra few dollars, the first thing I want to do is find something to buy with it.

Whether you're a spender like me, or a natural saver, we all need to be intentional with our money if we want to succeed at having any when we get older. As of this writing, the personal savings rate in America is 3.2%. That means for every $100 that the average person earns after taxes, they're saving $3.20. This includes retirement savings, emergency funds, and savings in general. 3.2% is an extremely low rate of savings, especially when you consider that most financial experts recommend saving at least 10-15% of your income just for retirement. You need to save because things happen in life that cost money. Cars break down, kids go to college, and you're going to retire someday.

We, as a country, are living very dangerously with our lack of savings. According to a 2016 GOBankingRates.com survey, 34% of Americans have absolutely no money in savings. Zero. If they were to have an emergency, they would have no responsible way to take care of it financially. 35% have less than $1,000 saved up. They, at least, would be able to cover small emergencies, but what if something major comes up?

Reasons to Save Money

There are three major reasons to save money: for emergencies, for purchases, and for retirement.

Emergencies

None of us like emergencies, especially financial ones. I don't know anyone who is excited because their basement was suddenly flooded and they have to shell out a thousand dollars for new carpeting.

Whether we like them or not, emergencies happen. That's why it's important to be financially prepared for them. It's not a question of whether an emergency will happen, but when. You could have a medical emergency that your insurance doesn't entirely cover, and have to shell out a couple thousand dollars out of pocket. This happened to me not long ago when I had to go to the emergency room because of some really scary symptoms where I thought I may be having a stroke (fortunately, it was nothing nearly that serious). I ended up having to pay over a thousand dollars out of pocket after all was said and done because the nearest hospital was out of network.

How about if you suddenly lose your job and have no income until you find something new? Finding a new job that you can make a similar or better salary at could take months, and during that timeframe you're still going to have bills to pay. The rent or mortgage will continue coming due each month, your family will need to eat, and you'll have to keep the lights on.

What if you had a natural disaster like a flood, tornado or hurricane hit your house? Depending on the circumstances and your coverage, your insurance policy may not cover the damage. You'll need money saved up to get back on your feet.

Before you do anything extra with your money after you pay your bills, you want to save up a starter emergency fund of $1,000. This will cover most minor emergencies and prevent you from turning to a credit card or a loan. Then, once you're out of consumer debt (all debt except the mortgage), you want to crank your emergency fund up to between three and six months of expenses. Note that I said expenses, not income. You're not looking to completely replace your income with this money, just the monthly expenses that will need covering in the case of a major emergency.

If you're single or you have a pretty stable job with consistent income, you can lean more toward the three-month side. On the other hand, if you have a family to support or if you work primarily on commission, I suggest saving six months of expenses. An emergency would be a bigger deal in that household, so your fund should be larger as well.

Remember, this money is only for emergencies! It should be fairly easy to access but resist the urge to touch it when you want to make impulsive purchases and save up money for those separately. You don't want to park this money in an investment account because you won't be able to access it easily when an emergency does arise. The ideal place for your emergency fund is in a simple money market account at your bank or credit union. If you're someone that has an impulsive nature, you may want to open an account somewhere other than your primary bank because you will be less likely to use it for non-emergencies.

Think of your emergency fund as an insurance policy. What do most of us do with insurance policies? We pay into them but hardly ever file claims. That's what you want to do with this money; put it in the account and don't touch it unless absolutely necessary.

Purchases

Your car is going to die. Maybe not today, maybe not even this year, but eventually the day will come when it will no longer work. What are you going to do when this happens? If you're like 90% of America, you'll go down to the dealership and take out a five or six year loan and be stuck with a payment of around $500 a month. Just writing that makes me twitch because I've been there.

I'm certainly not against having a nice car. I'm a car guy and am currently pining for the new Ford F-350 Super Duty pickup truck. If I wanted to, I could drive down to the Ford dealership right now, get a loan and be back home with it in a few hours. I'm not going to do that though. For one thing, that would make me a hypocrite and I practice what I preach. On a larger level, it would be a very poor financial decision. According to Carfax, a new car loses approximately 10% of its value the moment it is driven off the lot. After a year, it's lost another 10% on average and continues dropping from there.

Notice that I said "on average." Some brands fare worse than others. Take the Range Rover, for example. If you purchased a brand new one today, the sticker price starts at a little over $87,000. Five years later with average mileage of 12,000 per year, do you know how much that same car is worth (assuming it's in good condition)? **$39,891.** Your car has lost 55% of its value in five years.

Now I know that most people don't drive Range Rovers or even cars that expensive, but my point is that as a culture, we're sloppy when we buy cars. Most people don't purposefully go out and buy something that they know will go down 55% in value in five years. We don't think that far ahead. What if we started to, though? Go outside and look at how many miles are on your car. If you're in the six-digit range, you might want to get serious about setting some money aside both for future repairs and for the day that your car will no longer work. If you don't have that many miles on your car, that doesn't mean you're off the hook. Low-mileage cars die sometimes too. If yours isn't one of those, then you'll end up having more time to build up your next car fund but you will need it sooner or later. Why not be prepared?

Cars aren't the only major purchases we make. If you've been a homeowner for any length of time, you've probably discovered that appliances break and they're often expensive to replace. What about vacations? We all need a break from time to time and it's a lot better to have cash for that special trip than to put it on a credit card and be making payments on it months after you return. JetBlue came out with a program in 2017 where you can finance your vacation in 12 monthly installments with annual percentage rates that start at 8.99%. I mean, really? I have to hand it to JetBlue because they're probably going to make a killing on this. Please do not finance your vacation. I promise you will regret it.

Retirement

You're going to retire someday. How you do so is up to you. Most people have a dream of how they want their retirement to be spent, whether it's sitting on a beach soaking up the sun, traveling around the world to see exotic sights, or simply spending time with family and the grandkids. The problem is that kind of retirement doesn't happen without being intentional and putting in some work to make sure it can happen.

According to a recent Money magazine article, 56% of Americans have less than $10,000 saved for retirement and 33% have saved nothing. Nothing! You can't retire on that, at least not with dignity and without mooching off of everyone around you.

I have to admit, when I was in my 20s I gave no thought to retirement. I have plenty of time, I thought. I'll get serious about it when I get older. Let me tell you what a huge mistake that mindset was. When I started getting serious about turning my finances around, I discovered this little thing called compound interest. Only it's not a little thing, it's a HUGE thing, and it can be the difference between a mediocre retirement and an epic retirement depending on when you start saving.

One important thing I want to mention about retirement: you may not have a choice as to when you will retire. My parents found this out the hard way after suffering a myriad of health problems. They got to the point where they couldn't work anymore because their bodies would not let them, and they were not prepared for it at all. It's one of the scariest and most frustrating things a person can go through—wanting and needing to work to support yourself but not physically being able to. After witnessing the devastating effects this experience has had on my loved ones, I'm determined not to let it happen to me, which is why I make it a point to save a portion of each and every paycheck to go toward retirement. I will go more in-depth on retirement in a later chapter.

A Final Note

One thing to mention about saving money that will help you succeed at it: make sure you have a purpose for the money you save. If you're just saving money but have no reason or plan for it, you're either going to get bored and stop doing it or you're going to end up blowing it on something unnecessary. Know the reason why you are saving and you will stay on mission.

4

SPENDING

Homes, Cars & Other Major Purchases

Like I said, I've always been a natural spender. Ever since I was a kid, if I had money in my pocket I was determined to find a way to get rid of it. Eating out was (and still is) my number one way of spending, and I don't mean fine dining either. I may be a spender but I'm a cheap spender. I've rarely met a fast food restaurant I didn't like.

There's nothing wrong with being a spender if you're making a plan for it and spending within your means. We all want to enjoy life and buying things is one way of doing so. It's when people buy things they can't afford or borrow money because they just *have* to have something that it becomes an issue.

According to a 2016 survey done by payment processor TSYS, 40% of consumers prefer using a credit card for the majority of their purchases, an increase of 5% over the previous year. More than half of credit card holders say they use a credit card for everyday spending. A 2016 study done by FINRA showed that only 52% of credit card holders pay their card off every month. That means almost half of everyone out there with a credit card carries a balance on their card. The cost of doing this is high. The average annual percentage rate on a credit card with a balance was 13.51% in February 2016. So if you have a credit card with a $10,000 balance, you're paying over $1,300 in interest!

The point I'm trying to make here is that it is very easy to get out of control with your spending habits. We're constantly being marketed to and companies spend a huge amount of money on making sure you see their products and want to buy them—over $180 billion in 2017!

Businesses spend this much money because they know it works. Between billboards, television and internet advertising, and celebrity endorsements, you're going to see their product one way or another.

Real Estate

Owning your own home is part of the American dream. Most of us have a picture in our head of our dream home, whether it's on a lake, in the mountains, or just something comfortable in the suburbs. The process of home buying, however, can be overwhelming. *How do we know when the right time to buy is? What house should I buy? How do I go about it? And what are all these different mortgage options?* It can be difficult to sort through all the information being thrown at you, so let's go through the basics.

When Should I Buy a House?

This is the most important question to ask, because if you buy a home at the wrong time, you'll be setting yourself up for a financial disaster. Every month, tens of thousands of American houses are foreclosed on and many times it's because the owner wasn't in the right place financially when buying. Before you purchase a house, you want to have two things: NO debt and an emergency fund of 3-6 months of expenses saved up in addition to your down payment.

For your down payment, in an ideal situation you want to have at least 20% of the home cost saved up that you can put down. The main reason for this is to avoid having to purchase private mortgage insurance (PMI), which is required by law if you have less than 80% equity in your house. In some areas of the country, 20% is hard to come by and can take a considerable amount of time to save, so if you don't mind paying for PMI then you can buy at below the 20% threshold. Do not buy a home if you do not have at least 10% saved, however. This throws up warning flags that you are not ready yet and probably can't afford the house. Slow down and wait a little longer.

What House Should I Buy?

There are several factors to take into account when choosing a home. You never want to buy the most expensive house in a neighborhood. That will pretty much guarantee that it is overvalued and when it's time to sell, you won't make as much profit. You want to choose a good location. Find a home in a good neighborhood with good schools and preferably with a nice view. Properties near water usually appreciate well over time. You can also find bargains by looking for homes that don't have the ideal "look" but can be easily modified. For example, you can always change the landscaping, or replace ugly carpet or outdated wallpaper. Many people won't want to bother with these types of things but they are easy to fix and usually cheap.

What Do I Need to Know About the Process?

You always want to use a real estate agent. They have full access to the Multiple Listing Service (MLS) and it's much easier than trying to find a house on your own, not to mention that you will get a better deal than when you try to negotiate on your own. You can also use websites such as Zillow, but they shouldn't be your primary resource. Always have the house you want to buy inspected by a certified home inspector for mechanical and structural issues. Get the home appraised so you have an idea if you're overpaying. And make sure you get title insurance, which protects you in the case of an unclean title.

What Kind of Mortgage Do I Get?

The only type of mortgage I recommend is a 15-year fixed-rate loan. If you were to buy a $200,000 house with a 5% APR and a 20% down payment, for example, your monthly payment on a 30-year loan (which is the norm) would be $1,113 per month. If we switch that to a 15-year loan, you would think the payment would double, correct? Wrong. It only increases to $1,519 per month. Here's the kicker, though: you're going to pay over $80,000 more in interest with the 30-year loan. Why in the world would anyone want to do that? I sure wouldn't.

You also want to make sure that your monthly payment is no more than 25% of your take-home pay and as I stated before, put at least 10% down, if not 20%.

There are other types of mortgages out there but most of them you want to avoid. Adjustable-rate mortgages (ARMs), interest-only mortgages and reverse mortgages are all horrible options. FHA and VA loans are not great either. You'd think they would be since their purpose is to help out potential buyers in less than ideal circumstances, but they are riddled with high fees that make them undesirable.

You also don't want to sign up for any accelerated or bi-weekly payoff programs unless you can do so at no charge. Most of those programs charge you extra to do something that you can do on your own for free which will enable you to pay off your mortgage early.

Yes, you want to pay your mortgage off early. Once you start saving for retirement and for your children's college (if you choose to), you want to throw any extra money you have at paying off the house early. I want to forewarn you, however, that there will be people that will try to talk you into keeping your mortgage for the tax benefits. The problem with that, however, is it doesn't make mathematical sense. If you have a $200,000 mortgage with a 5% interest rate, you would be paying $10,000 a year in interest so you can avoid paying $2,500 in taxes. How is that a benefit?

Automobiles

I've learned quite a bit over the years from mistakes I and other people have made with car purchases. Here are four of them:

1. Do not buy a brand new car.

Seriously, unless you have a net worth of at least a million dollars, it's unwise to buy a new car. Most cars depreciate 60-70% in the first four years of existence, which means you are losing a ton of money just by driving it off the lot. Obviously someone has to buy all these new cars, but don't let it be you. Buying a new car is like flushing a hundred-dollar bill down your toilet once a week. Most millionaires don't even drive brand new cars. According to the book *The Millionaire Next Door* by Thomas Stanley, the average millionaire drives a slightly-used, two or three year old car that they bought with cash.

2. Do not finance your car.

There are a lot of people out there that are absolutely convinced that car payments are a way of life and the only way to drive a nice car. It's one of the biggest lies out there and one that is financially destroying millions of families. I succumbed to this for almost 15 years and let me tell you, once I gave it up it was so freeing not having a car payment (and actually having some money in my bank account!). Only buy a car with the amount of money that you actually have at the time. This means you are going to have to start a savings fund for your next car so that you're prepared when that time comes (and don't forget about taxes and registration fees).

3. Do not lease your car.

Leasing is the most expensive way to operate a car. Car dealers make more money on leases than anything else (except repairs). Leasing is a way that middle-class people can drive new BMWs and Mercedes-Benz's that they can't afford to buy. In fact, a study done by HIS Markit showed that 76% of new Mercedes-Benz vehicles sold in NYC and Los Angeles were leases! Also, for those of you who claim that you lease your car for the tax advantages, you can get those same advantages on a car you actually own.

4. Do not buy an extended warranty.

87% of the cost of an extended warranty goes to commission, overhead, and profit for the company selling it. Basically, if you just saved 13% of the cost of the warranty in your bank account, you could pay cash for most repairs that pop up. Every vehicle has a problem at some point, but extended warranties are rip-offs. You put way more money in than you'll ever get out of it.

Making Wise Purchase Decisions

When making a major purchase, there are things you can do to help yourself get your money's worth. The most important advice I can give is to never buy on impulse with any item greater than $100. Wait at least 24 hours to think it over and do a quick Google search to see if you can find a better deal. Nowadays you can comparison shop very easily online and most of the time you will find a better deal if you just take a few minutes to look around. Check out garage sales or Craigslist to see if you can find a gently-used item for a deal. Purchase your local newspaper to see if there are any auctions, estate sales or repossession sales going on in your area. There are plenty of deals out there if you just look around!

5

Retirement

How to Make Sure the Golden Years Stay Golden

Ah, retirement: The day when you won't have to get in your car and fight traffic to get to a job that you may hate. *Wow Shane, that sounds pessimistic.* Maybe it is, but it's a reality for a lot of people. 70% of Americans, according to a recent Gallup poll, are either not engaged at their jobs or downright hate them.

Some of us can't wait for retirement. Others are dreading the thought, not because they don't want to be retired, but because they know they're not financially prepared for it. One thing is for sure though: every one of us will face retirement one day. It will either be because we decided it was time and we're financially ready, or because we're at a point in our lives where we physically can't work any longer and retirement is forced upon us.

According to another Gallup poll, the average American expects to retire at age 66 but actually ends up retiring at 62. 49% of those people said it was out of their control due to unforeseen circumstances. Out of those people, 61% were forced to retire due to a disability or health condition and 18% retired to care for a spouse or other family member. Only 26% of people retired early because they became financially able to do so earlier than expected.

Retirement in America Today

Retirement itself is a relatively modern concept. Prior to the late nineteenth century, the vast majority of people worked until they died. A lot of it was related to the fact that people rarely lived to old age because of the lack of modern medicine and amenities. Fortunately, we have come a long way since then.

As we dig into the topic of retirement, here are some terms you may have heard of.

Pensions

In 1889, German Chancellor Otto von Bismarck introduced what we now know as the modern pension system, which continued to pay a portion of a worker's salary after they had been working for a certain amount of time. At the time, a retired worker might live for 10 to 15 years at most after leaving the job, so it was doable for many companies to offer pensions to their employees.

Nowadays due to the advance of modern medicine, a person could potentially live 20 to 30 years after retiring. The cost for companies to continue offering pensions has grown to astronomical proportions, so now in the 21st century, they are extremely rare.

401(k)s, IRAs & Other Retirement Plans

Most of us are familiar with the terms 401(k) and IRA. If not, I will explain it for you. The 401(k) came about from legislative acts written in the 1970s that established how retirement plans can legally work and the rules that must be followed. The name 401(k) actually comes from the section of the tax code that spells out the guidelines for how it works.

In a nutshell, a 401(k) is a retirement plan offered by your employer where you are responsible for saving your own money for retirement. In a traditional 401(k), the money that you put into the account is deposited before taxes are taken out of your paycheck, so your taxable income is decreased because of this. In addition to the money that you save into this account, many employers offer a match up to a certain percentage. This is essentially free money, which is a great deal!

Some of you may have a different plan offered through your workplace, such as a 403(b) or a 457 plan. These work the same way as 401(k) plans but are just offered by certain types of employers. 403(b) plans are usually offered for employees of public schools, certain tax-exempt organizations, and ministers. 457 plans are usually offered to government employees.

An IRA is a retirement account that you can open on your own through a bank or brokerage firm and is independent of your employer. IRA stands for Individual Retirement Arrangement. IRAs work the same way as a 401(k), only without the potential match.

Social Security

The Social Security program is the major reason why most people think that the retirement age is 65 today. This government program, instated by the Social Security Act of 1935, was a way to provide income for retired Americans starting at the age of 65. When it was developed, most people didn't live much longer than 60 so it made sense that there would be money available for those who lived past the 65 year mark. Today, the average life expectancy in America is 79 for men and 81 for women. Do you see the problem? There's not enough money there to support everyone retiring today.

Today, the age to qualify for full Social Security benefits is on the rise. For someone in their thirties like me, the age has risen to 67. Even with the age increase, the program is paying out a lot more money than it's taking in. Based on a report by the Social Security Administration in 2015, the fund is on track to be depleted by 2034, at which point it will only be able to pay out 79% of scheduled benefits from ongoing tax revenue. This represents a huge problem if you plan to rely on Social Security when you retire.

Developing a Game Plan

You don't want to rely on Social Security in your retirement, that's for sure. This means that you're going to have to come up with a solid plan so that you have enough money to retire comfortably. For starters, let's forget about the whole "retire at 65" notion. That's the government's outdated plan for you. Since they're not going to be paying for your retirement, they shouldn't be the ones telling you when you can do it. So when can you do it? Here is how to develop a game plan for planning your retirement.

Get Rid of Debt

Having debt is the number one roadblock that will derail your retirement dreams. Staying in debt prior to retirement is going to make it that much harder to save up a large amount of money for retirement. Once you do retire, if you continue to remain in debt by buying things you can't afford, you're going to be disappointed when you aren't able to keep the same standard of living you were used to having during your working life.

In case you glossed over that last statement, let me be perfectly clear: *you do not want to carry debt into retirement*—not even a mortgage. Car loans are even worse. In the previous chapter, I explained why car loans are horrible but they're even worse in retirement. Don't do it to yourself because you will regret it.

Have an Emergency Fund

Once you're out of consumer debt, meaning you've paid off everything except the house, the next thing you want to do is stock up cash. A good amount to have on hand in a savings or money market account is between three and six months of expenses. You want this money to be liquid and easy to access for when emergencies happen. When your car breaks down or you have a medical emergency that isn't completely covered by insurance, you will need somewhere to turn to other than a credit card or a loan. This savings account is your answer to these hiccups in life.

Sinking Funds

A sinking fund is basically a special savings account for specific large purchases that we know will be coming up in the near future. These are things like car replacement, vacations, foreseeable home repairs such as knowing that your roof will need to be replaced soon, and even some smaller purchases like a mattress that is starting to get worn out and will need to be replaced soon.

Sinking funds are used to pay for things that are *not* emergencies. This is because we know that they are coming sooner or later and we want to be prepared. If your car has 100,000 miles on it, now would be a good time to start a sinking fund so you can replace it when it dies.

Save 15% of Your Income for Retirement

When you're out of debt and have a savings account of three to six months of expenses, the next thing you want to do is set aside 15% of your gross income specifically for retirement. This is when you want to open up one or more of those retirement accounts that I talked about. If your employer offers a plan, such as a 401(k), 403(b) or 457, you want to start there especially if a match is offered. I recommend contributing up to the amount of the match and then switching over to an IRA. This is because you will have a lot more investment options in an IRA than you will in an employer-sponsored plan. The average employer-sponsored plan has twenty-five different investment choices, while in an IRA you have thousands.

Roth IRAs and 401(k)s

Traditional retirement accounts take contributions pre-tax, meaning before you are taxed on it. The tax is deferred, and you do not pay those taxes until you withdraw the money at retirement. That sounds good except for one problem: the vast majority of people are in a higher tax bracket at retirement, so they end up paying a lot more in taxes.

Enter the Roth. What a Roth IRA or Roth 401(k) does is allow you to contribute after-tax income to your retirement account, which allows it to grow tax-free until you take it out at retirement. You have already paid taxes on that money so you're off the hook! Also, since it's growing tax free over a period of twenty, thirty, or more years (depending on when you start investing), you will have a lot more money by using the Roth option than you would in a traditional IRA or 401(k). If you have the option, *ALWAYS* choose the Roth.

How to Invest

Now that we've gone over the basics of retirement accounts and when to start investing, let's move onto how you should invest your money. As I said earlier, once you're out of debt and have an emergency fund of three to six months of expenses saved up, next you want to start saving 15% of your gross income specifically for retirement. Sounds simple enough, but now we're going to get into the nitty-gritty of what to do with that money. There are a lot of options; some of them are good and others should be avoided.

CDs, Bonds & Single Stocks

When I talk about CDs, I don't mean those circular discs from the nineties that play music. I'm talking about Certificates of Deposit, which are basically bank accounts with a certificate that says you put your money in the bank and you're going to leave it there for the length of time they designate. There's a problem with CDs, however, and it's that they give you virtually no rate of return on your money. The average rate of return on a 5-year CD as of this writing is slightly over 1%. That's lower than inflation and even some savings accounts. The worst part is that your money is locked into the account for the length of time designated by the CD.

Bonds are loans that you, the investor, are making to a company or government that they promise to pay back in full with interest. The federal government, for example, sells bonds to individuals to finance its debts. There are different types of bonds but I'll save you the trouble of researching them by telling you not to waste your time with them. Despite popular belief, bonds are not risk-free and they do not give great rates of return. Plus, if you want to cash a bond in prior to its maturity, you won't get all of your money back.

When you buy a single stock, you are buying a piece of a company. You're entitled to a share of any profits that the company makes and you get to participate in some of the decision-making for the company. The price of a stock is driven by the performance of that company, so if the company is making a lot of money, the price will go up. If the company is doing poorly, the price will go down. In theory, it sounds simple: if you choose to invest in the stocks of good companies, you will make money. The problem with that, however, is that single stocks are very volatile. A reputable and profitable company could have a condemning news story come out about them and instantly, the stock price could plummet, causing you to lose a ton of money. You don't know when, or even if, you will make that money back.

Mutual Funds

The only long-term investment I personally choose, and I encourage you to do the same, is mutual funds. Mutual funds are investments that pool your money together with other investors to buy shares of a portfolio comprised of stocks, bonds, or other securities. Every mutual fund has a manager, who chooses the funds that comprise the portfolio. There are a variety of different types of mutual funds that have different objectives. The four most common ones are large-cap (also called growth and income funds), mid-cap (also called growth funds), small-cap (also called aggressive growth funds), and overseas or international funds.

Large-cap funds represent large companies (valued over $10 billion) that you've probably heard of, such as Apple, Walmart and McDonald's. Mid-cap funds represent medium size companies (valued between $2 billion and $10 billion), and small-cap funds represent smaller companies (valued at less than $2 billion). If you're buying a large-cap mutual fund, for example, you're buying shares in a group of large companies.

The reason I want you to invest in mutual funds, rather than single stocks, is because there is stability in large groups. With a single stock, the value will go up and down significantly based on the day-to-day happenings within a company. If you own a share of a mutual fund, however, you have a lot of companies in that fund to help each other out. If a couple of stocks in your fund have a bad day, you have other ones to help absorb the drop and you won't lose as much money. The overall value of the fund should go up over time, which gives you a positive return in investment.

When choosing your mutual funds, I recommend that you choose well-performing funds from several different categories. By doing so, you will have a well-rounded portfolio that will grow steadily over time.

What do I mean by well-performing? Let's put it this way: the average annual return of the S&P 500 since 1928 is 11.85%. Since the S&P 500 represents the 500 largest companies in America, I would say that's a pretty good standard to go by. By simply investing in an index fund that tracks the S&P 500, you could achieve this. But what if I told you that you could do better?

It really isn't that hard to find well-performing mutual funds. In a couple minutes you can pull up a list of funds in different categories online, and then you would need to run a filter to weed out the ones you don't want. The key thing to look for is long-term performance of at least ten years and preferably fifteen. You want to invest in funds that have been around for a long time, as that shows they are stable and are more likely to make you money.

A lot of financial "professionals" will argue that it's impossible to get a 12% return. I disagree, and I have proof. In my personal Roth IRA account, I am currently investing in four different funds that have ten-year returns of 13.66%, 20.56%, 11.41%, and 16.03%. That gives my portfolio an average annual return of 15.42%, which beats the S&P 500. So yes, it can be done.

The Power of Compound Interest

If you haven't heard of compound interest yet, I'm about to blow your mind. Albert Einstein once said that compound interest is the eighth wonder of the world. It can make you a millionaire, even if you're an average Joe, and especially if you start investing while you're young.

To illustrate the power of compound interest, let's say you invest $1,000 and then get a 10% return on your investment at the end of the year. That gives you $1,100. After another year, you obtained another 10% return. Only you're not just getting a return on your original $1,000, you're earning interest on your interest as well. Now you have $1,210, and that's without even investing any additional money. Imagine what can be achieved over a 40-year period where you're continually investing. A 25-year old making $50,000 per year and investing 10% of his income could have over $2.4 million at age 65, and that's without even getting a raise during his career! That's why it's important to start investing early and to leave the money alone once it's in the account.

It's Your Retirement!

Lastly, and most importantly, make sure you have a plan for when you're retired. Not just for your money, but for your life. What do you want to be doing when you're retired? Do you want to travel the world? Do you want to spend a lot of time with the grandkids? Do you want to volunteer and help people? Retirement looks different for everyone, so it's important to know what you want yours to look like. You get to decide that, and if you start financially planning for it early enough, you'll be able to do just about anything you want. Start now!

6

KIDS, COLLEGE & PRIORITIZING
A.K.A. How to NOT Wreck Your Retirement Plans

If you've ever flown on an airplane, you know the drill right before the plane takes off from the runway. One of the flight attendants gets on the loudspeaker, tells you to buckle up, and goes over the safety information. Do you remember the part about the proper procedures for oxygen masks? Make sure you put on *YOUR* oxygen mask first before helping the person next to you. That tiny bit of information can save a life. Why? Because you can't help someone else if you don't take care of yourself first.

This bit of advice comes into play with your finances as well, and can be the difference between retiring with dignity and having to rely on your children in your later years. Trust me, you don't want the latter. According to the National Student Clearinghouse Research Center, only 55% of college students graduate. 100% of us will retire one way or another.

I'm certainly not saying that your child shouldn't go to college. I *am* saying that it shouldn't come before saving for retirement. There are several ways that your child can go to college without you sacrificing your golden years, and I will go over them in this chapter. First, however, let's look at some hard truths about college.

1. A college degree does not ensure a well-paying job.

There is a big misconception in America today that going to college will ensure that you will get a high-paying job and you will be financially set for life. I'll tell you right now—it's a lie. First off, 38% of college graduates are working in a job that doesn't even require a degree and 73% are in a job that has absolutely nothing to do with their major. I personally know several of them. A college degree may help you get your foot in the door for an interview but it will not ensure any job.

2. A college degree does not ensure that you will be successful.

Ellen DeGeneres, Ted Turner, Russell Simmons, Steve Jobs, Michael Dell, John Rockefeller. What do these people all have in common? They either never went or never graduated from college. They're also highly successful. A 2006 study done by Accenture of 251 executives in six countries showed that the biggest personal trait that determines success is emotional intelligence. These are things such as how you relate to others, self-awareness and social awareness—all way more important than a college degree.

3. Going to an expensive private college will not give you an advantage over state schools.

How many times have we heard someone bragging about going to an Ivy League school? I know I have. Does it really matter, though? A Gallup survey taken in 2014 asking college graduates how they were doing across five different metrics, including financially, physically and socially, showed that 11% of public college graduates were thriving. Private college graduates? 12%. A bigger predictor of whether a college graduate is thriving was whether or not he or she had student loans, which with a more expensive private school education is more likely.

No, I'm not against college.

At this point, you're probably thinking, wow, Shane really is against people going to college. No, I'm not. I *am* against people making all kinds of ridiculous and unnecessary sacrifices to go to college thinking that it's going to solve all of your problems when it isn't. If you think that way then there is a huge chance you are going to be let down. College is a great thing and has all kinds of life benefits, but it's not for everyone, and it's certainly not worth wrecking your retirement over when you can't afford it. I do want your child to go to college, so let me show you how to do it the right way.

5 Ways Your Child Can Go to College without Derailing Your Retirement

College is expensive. According to CollegeData.com, the average cost for tuition and fees for the 2016-17 school year was $9,650 for in-state tuition at a public college, $24,930 for out-of-state tuition at a public college, and $33,480 for private college tuition. Multiply that by four years (and the average college student is actually taking six years to complete a bachelor's degree nowadays), and that's a huge sum of money. Fortunately, there are ways to handle this without breaking the bank or dooming you to a retirement of living on Social Security.

Tax-Free Savings Accounts

There are a few different options to save for college tax-free. The first program you want to check out is the Education Savings Account, or ESA. It's similar to a Roth IRA in that you invest after-tax money in it and it grows tax-free. As of this writing, the current contribution limit is $2,000 per year. If you start this account when your child is born and select well-performing mutual funds, as I detailed in the previous chapter, this account could grow to over $100,000 by the time your child turns 18. That will take care of four years of college for just about everyone unless you are going to a very expensive private college. There is an income limit that you must meet to use an ESA, however. Currently that sits at $190,000 per year for married couples filing joint tax returns, or $110,000 for a single filer.

The next plan you want to check out is the 529 plan. This plan does not have contribution or income limits, so if you make too much money for an ESA or you want to save more than $2,000 per year, this is the best plan for you. Be cautious of the plan you select, however. Some of them give you little or no control over the mutual funds that are selected, which can leave you with low annual returns. Only select a 529 plan where you can pick and choose the investments you're investing in.

A third option, which I'm not crazy about, is the Uniform Transfers/Gifts to Minors Act (UTMA or UGMA). This plan allows you to save for college at a reduced rate, but the downside is that once the child turns 21 (for an UTMA) or 18 (for an UGMA), they are allowed to take the money and do whatever they want with it, even if it's not education-related. That may work out alright if you have a responsible young adult that makes wise choices, but if that person has become an out-of-control partier or a drug addict, you're basically giving them a blank check to blow. It's not worth the risk in my opinion.

Scholarships

Scholarships are gifts of free money awarded to students to pay for all or part of their education. Most of them are merit-based, meaning the student has to have earned it for some reason. There are many different types of scholarships and they can be given for reasons such as athletic prowess, excellent grades, community work, or even based on your demographics. According to CollegeRaptor.com, 57% of all financial aid comes from scholarships or grants, and over $122 billion was awarded in scholarships or grants across the U.S. during the 2013-14 school year. What's even more interesting is that only 13% of scholarships come from private sources, meaning either the government or colleges are the ones offering the vast majority of them.

As I looked into the different reasons scholarships have been given over the past ten years, I found some interesting (and strange) scholarships out there. Did you know there is a scholarship just for being tall? I also found a scholarship for talented skateboarders, and the weirdest one I came across was a scholarship for being good at drawing pictures of ducks!

Just to throw a few more statistics out there, over 177 thousand athletic scholarships are given every year that are worth over $1 billion. McDonald's, KFC, Dr. Pepper and Coca-Cola combined give students over $5.5 million is scholarships every year. You want to know what's sad though? Over $100 million of potential scholarships go unclaimed every year in the United States. This would cover the full cost of tuition for 14,000 additional students.

If you are a senior in high school, please make it your full-time job to apply for as many scholarships as you can. You will probably get turned down for most of them but if you apply for a lot, you will get some and it will be worth your time.

Grants

One of the first things you should do when you or your child is getting ready to go to college is fill out the FAFSA, which stands for Free Application for Federal Student Aid. This application will put you in the system for different types of financial aid, which includes government grants. Grants come from a variety of sources, including states, corporations and other private institutions, but the largest amount of them come from the federal government.

Grants come in two different categories: need-based and merit-based. Need-based grants are what they sound like: grants given to those who have the greatest financial need. Merit-based grants are given for exceptional performance—things like exceptional grades and other personal achievements.

Like scholarships, grants do not have to be repaid. There are a variety of grants that target different segments of the student population, such as children in foster care, students with disabilities, and children of veterans or National Guard members. A few of the most popular grants are the Pell Grant, the SMART Grant, and the Academic Competitiveness Grant.

Federal grant programs are funded by Congress, so maximum awards and availability vary from year to year. Some are distributed on a first-come first-serve basis, so you want to fill out your FAFSA as early as possible.

Work

Yes, it is possible to work your way through school. I know several people who literally worked a full-time job while going to school full-time and graduated debt-free. You will have to find a job that you can work your school schedule around and that pays more than minimum wage, but it can be done. Also, your young adult should be working as much as he or she can over summer break, not lounging around or going on endless vacations. It won't kill them and five or ten years down the road after they graduate they will be very thankful that they did. I have a friend who mowed lawns when he was home for the summer and made enough money to cover his whole tuition for the following school year, and he would do this every summer while he was in college. Granted, he worked about 12 hours a day, 6 days a week, but he sacrificed his social life for a few years because he was on a mission and ended up achieving it.

Start at Community College

There is nothing wrong with starting out at a community college. Many of them are very highly rated and give great educations. The best part is that you can save a ton of money by sending Junior to a community college for the first two years. The average in-state tuition at a community college for the 2017-18 school year was $4,868. Even if you live in a state where it's a bit higher, it's still a whole lot cheaper than a four-year school. Once you finish the first two years and transfer, you're still getting a bachelor's degree from the four-year school and nobody will know the difference!

What If I Still Just Don't Have the Money?

Then now is not the best time for you or your child to go to college. Put it off for a year or two while you save up, and then reconsider. Chances are, in that time period, you may reconsider whether college is even necessary. You or your child could find an awesome job that you love and pays a decent income, and suddenly college may not be so important after all.

Student Loans—The New Four Letter Word

I'm saving the most important section of all for last in this chapter, and I cannot emphasize this enough. Do not, under any circumstance, take out a student loan or allow your child to do so. Ever! They will follow you around for what seems like forever. They are not dischargeable in a bankruptcy and the average person takes 21 years to pay them off. That's more than some mortgages. According to a study done by Forbes magazine, the average student in the class of 2016 owes $37,172 in student loan debt, with the average payment being $351 per month. All of that when there is only a 55% chance you will graduate and a 62% chance that you will work in a job that requires a degree!

Like I said at the beginning of this chapter, I am not against college, not even a little bit. I am against making rash decisions and when it comes down to it, taking out a student loan is a lot like gambling. You're taking a huge gamble with a lot of money on a degree that may or may not pay off. If you have the money to pay for it upfront or have a plan to pay for it without using debt, then go to college. If not, then now is not the time for you. I'm not saying to never go—I'm just saying don't do it right now. Student loan debt is now the second highest debt category—only behind mortgage debt, and it's causing a lot of intense stress in people's lives. People are getting divorced and are even committing suicide over it. Just don't do it.

7

Insurance

What You Need and What You Don't

I know what you're thinking. A chapter about insurance...oh boy...this will be good reading when I'm trying to fall asleep at night. I'll admit that the topic of insurance can be a bit boring at times. I never gave it much thought until a few years ago when it hit home for me.

Ever since I was a kid, my father had been a hard worker. Coming from a military family, he lived in a lot of different places around the country and even spent a few years in Germany as a kid. Not long before I was born, my parents settled down in Tucson, Arizona, where my father embarked in a career in mechanical engineering which he learned from the ground up. He didn't have a degree but he did have a strong work ethic and did what it took to put food on the table for our family.

After about twenty-five years in the engineering field, my dad got laid off when the company he worked for downsized. He attempted to find another job in his field but times were changing, engineering was evolving, and he couldn't keep up with all the changes. He was also in his fifties at this point and kept getting passed over in interviews for younger applicants.

What transpired over the next ten years was truly a tragic tale. My father never gave up working, and would take whatever job he could find no matter how menial it was. He worked in a video editing store for several years making less than half of what he used to make, and also delivered newspapers and takeout food at night to make ends meet. This was until his health started failing and at the age of sixty he was forced to retire, as his body could no longer handle the physical labor.

After having a stroke, being diagnosed with Type 2 diabetes, and losing a leg and half a foot to amputation due to gangrene, the medical bills started pouring in. Two long-term stays in nursing homes racked up a debt of over $100,000. It took close to two years to convince the Social Security Administration that he was, in fact, disabled and couldn't work before he was approved for disability income and Medicare since he wasn't 65 yet. My dad had gone through all of his savings by this point to stay afloat and there was nothing left.

I tell this story to help everyone realize the need for insurance. Throughout all of this, my father didn't have a single insurance policy in place, which exacerbated his financial problems exponentially. Now I know that there are some things insurance doesn't cover and that it may not have solved every single problem completely, but it would have made a world of difference.

Let's go over the insurance options we have, because there are a lot of them. Some policies are essential, while others are just gimmicks and a waste of money. I want to make sure you get the most for your money and only buy what you need. Here we go!

Insurance Policies Everyone Needs

Term Life Insurance

If you have a family, and especially if you are the main breadwinner, you need to have life insurance. Life insurance replaces your income when you die. If you have a spouse and kids that count on that income to survive, life insurance ensures that in the event you pass away they will be able to eat and that your spouse doesn't have to panic wondering how to feed the kids on top of grieving.

There are two main types of life insurance: term and cash value (sometimes known as whole life). When you buy term insurance, you're buying an insurance policy for a specific term. The policy does one thing—it pays the face amount to the beneficiary of your choosing when you die. Frankly, that's all you need it to do.

Cash value insurance is a plan that you purchase that lasts the rest of your life. Not only are you buying insurance, but you're also putting money into a savings account inside the insurance policy. A lot of insurance agents will try to tell you that this is an investment but it's a load of malarkey. If you are investing in good mutual funds, like I explained in a previous chapter, you can make over 10% on your money easily. The average return on investment in a cash value insurance policy is between 3 and 6%. How is that a wise investment? Oh, and I haven't mentioned the worst part: when you die, your beneficiary only gets the face value of the policy. All of that extra money you saved up in the "investment" is kept by the insurance company!

The only life insurance policy I recommend is a term policy. It's significantly cheaper for a lot more coverage. If you are married and/or have children, you want to buy a policy that covers ten times your annual income. This will take care of your family after you're gone and give everyone peace of mind.

Health Insurance

With medical debt being the leading cause of bankruptcy, health insurance is a necessity. According to the Census Bureau, however, 8.8% of Americans did not have health insurance in 2016. This can be for a wide variety of reasons and affordability is a large factor for people of lower income, but with the implementation of the Affordable Care Act, it is becoming easier.

If you are someone who does not have coverage through your job, there are ways to make coverage more affordable. The first thing you can do is have a high deductible. Yes, you are taking on more risk but your monthly premium will be lower in return. If you have an emergency fund with three to six months of expenses saved up like I recommend, you should be able to do this.

Another way to save money on health expenses is to have a Health Savings Account (HSA). This is basically a tax-sheltered savings account for medical expenses when you have a high deductible. Your money grows tax-free, can be used for any medical expense, and also rolls over from year to year. The government also lets you write off the contributions you make to it. HSAs aren't ideal for everyone, however. They're great if you're extremely healthy or extremely sick, but if you're somewhere in the middle, it may not be worth it.

Car Insurance

You would think that just about everyone who drives has car insurance but recent statistics show that 14% of motorists are driving uninsured. Aside from the fact that this is illegal in most states, it's extremely unwise financially. If you were to get in an accident where you are at fault, you are personally liable for any damages that occur, which is a quick way to bankruptcy. When shopping for a policy, make sure you know what the legal limits are for coverage in your state. Regardless of your legal limit, you always want to have at least $500,000 liability coverage. This could save you from bankruptcy if you're at fault in a major accident.

To keep your premium down, select a higher deductible. Most people choose either a $250 or $500 deductible because they don't want to shell out the money if they were to get in an accident, but how often do you really get in accidents? Statistics show that the average person only files a collision claim once every 18 years.

I have a $1,000 deductible on my policy and recommend you do the same. Yes, it's a lot of money but if you're only paying it once every 18 years on average, it's worth it. You could save a lot of money each month.

Long-Term Disability Insurance

Did you know that if you're under age 35, you have a 33% chance of becoming disabled for at least six months at some point in your career? You're also twelve times more likely to become disabled than die by age 65. That makes disability insurance a necessity. When looking for a policy, you want to stick with long-term, not short (that's what your emergency fund is for). This will cover anything over a five-year period. The best place to buy it is through your workplace, but you can get it as an individual as well. I have an individual policy and it costs me about $40 per month.

Homeowner's or Renter's Insurance

This will cover your belongings in the case of a disaster in your home. The key to keeping premiums down, again, is to get a higher deductible. This will be a big savings in the long run, even if you do have a few claims. Renter's insurance is extremely affordable and necessary, since your landlord or apartment's insurance policy will not cover your belongings.

Long-Term Care Insurance

This will cover nursing home or assisted-living facility stays, as well as in-home care. You want to buy a long-term care policy when you turn 60. Statistically, it is a waste of money before that time and very expensive if you wait until after 60 to get a policy. Americans are living longer than ever and the cost of medical treatment is going up daily. According to the American Association of Homes and Services for the Aging, 69% of people turning 65 today will need some form of long-term care, however only 10% of seniors have long-term care insurance. That means the rest of them will be paying these astronomical costs out of pocket or going bankrupt.

Identity Theft Insurance

Identity theft is the fastest growing white-collar crime in America today. If you're a victim of it, it's very time-consuming to clean up as well. That's why identity theft insurance is a must. When looking for a policy, you want to make sure that it provides restoration services if your identity is stolen. That means that the insurance company will be doing all the work to fix the mess so that you don't have to. There are a lot of bad policies out there that don't do much of anything, so make sure you shop around for a good one. Good identity theft insurance is extremely cheap so there's no reason not to have it.

One Last Thing

Aside from insurance, there is one more thing that every single person needs to have: a will. According to LexisNexis, approximately 55% of Americans die without having a will in place. This puts an enormous strain on your family after you're gone, as they will have to go through the courts to determine what will happen to anything you may have and it can take years. Plus, in the end, the state will be the one to decide who gets your stuff, not you. How fair is that? I know death is a taboo topic that a lot of people don't want to talk or think about, but let's face it: the human race has a 100% mortality rate. We are all going to die at some point, so we should be prepared for it.

8

GIVING

Because It's Not All About You

Growing up, and even through most of my twenties, I have to admit I was a pretty selfish person in a lot of ways. As a child, I was told that it was nice to give but it was never really something that was emphasized. One thing that stands out in my teenage years, however, was when I wanted to get a job delivering newspapers but was too young at the time so my dad got the job and took me with him every morning before school. We did the paper route together and agreed to split the money, but at the end of the year-long period he gave me 100% of the money that we earned together. It was incredibly generous of him and I look back on that experience with fond memories.

American culture also contributed to my selfishness. Perhaps you have heard of the phrase, "The American Dream." Merriam-Webster defines it as "a happy way of living that is thought of by many Americans as something that can be achieved by anyone in the U.S. especially by working hard and becoming successful." At face value, that doesn't sound so bad. Who doesn't want a happy way of living? Most people want to work hard. Almost everyone wants to become successful.

When you think about it, however, the American Dream is all about you (and me!). We work hard and become successful so that we can be happy. We're chasing a moving target, because once you get to a point where you think you're happy, you start thinking of ways that you can be even happier. It's how the human mind works, and I know I've done it.

One of the first things I figured out after becoming a Christian at the age of 32 was that it's not about me. Not even a little bit. Now you may not have the same faith as me, but regardless of your personal beliefs there is a large weight that is lifted off your shoulders when you take the focus off of achieving the American Dream and take a look at the world around you. When you do this, you start to notice things. The first thing I noticed was how incredibly materialistic many of us are. The next thing you see is that people really have a need for approval. They want to be noticed and validated. People purchase cars worth six figures and handbags worth five figures for what reason? Usually to impress the people around them. It was the reason I went and bought a $20,000 car when I was 19 years old and couldn't afford it.

If you take an even deeper look at the world around you, you'll notice a third thing. People are hurting. There are homeless people, people with chronic illnesses, people with mental illness, disabled people, and people who have lost all hope that things will ever get better. There are people who need help, and they're not all that different than you or me. We should help them.

How I Became a Giver

As a young adult struggling with contentment and also not making a ton of money, giving money of any amount was not something I did. My attitude was that I worked hard for my money and had bills to pay, so why should I give it away? That would be counter-productive, my closed-mind thought. It all changed once I accepted Jesus as my Lord and Savior and started studying the Bible. Things really changed for me once I read Malachi 3:10, which states, "Bring the full tithe into the storehouse, that there may be food in my house. And thereby put me to the test, says the Lord of hosts, if I will not open the windows of heaven for you and pour down for you a blessing until there is no more need."

I had heard about giving ten percent of your income to the church before, but I had always glossed over it while thinking, "Yeah, right, like I can afford that." When I read Malachi 3:10, however, I had to make a decision. Was I going to be all in as a Christian, or just pick and choose the parts of the Bible that I want to follow? Hesitantly, I chose to test out the whole tithing thing, as the verse said, and gave ten percent of my next paycheck to my church.

I fully expected to financially struggle over the next two weeks until I got paid again, but something funny happened. *I was fine.* More than that, I actually had twenty dollars come to me unexpectedly. I couldn't believe it. It was as if God was saying, "See, I told you so." From that day on, I never failed to tithe to my local church, and I have never regretted it.

Now before I lose all of the non-Christian readers out there, my purpose of that story was simply to tell how I became a giver. If you don't believe in God, or follow another religion, that is your prerogative. I do think you will have a similar experience, however, if you start giving for the first time. You will discover that the sky will not start falling and your life will go on.

What Do You Want to Be Known For?

Winston Churchill once said, "We make a living by what we get, but we make a life by what we give." There's an important question that we all need to ask ourselves: What do I want to be known for? Believe it or not, you have the ability to have an enormous impact on the world around you. You get to choose what that is. We hear stories in the news every day about people who are unbelievably generous with both their time and their money and are doing great things for humanity. We also hear other stories about people who make huge impacts on the world, but for not-so-great reasons such as scamming people out of millions of dollars or being a drug kingpin who has killed thousands with their illicit products.

    The third type of person is the one who I feel the saddest for, and that's the person who doesn't really do much of anything of importance with their life. I'm not talking about being famous or a celebrity, but being a person who lives a life of mediocrity and is content with just getting by. That to me is the ultimate failure because every one of us has the innate capability to make a difference in the world in one way or another. You may or may not ever make a high income, but you can still do a lot to help people. You can be generous with your time and your abilities. There are many organizations that have a dire need for volunteers so that they can achieve their objectives and I believe that every one of us has a responsibility to do what we can to better this world.

Re-think your American Dream. Do you really want to spend your life acquiring "stuff"? I spent over a decade of my adult life doing that and it left me disappointed and feeling like a rat in a wheel because once you acquire that thing you always wanted, you will move onto something else. It's a never-ending cycle. Do I have it perfect? Absolutely not. I still struggle with materialism from time to time and once I realize what I'm doing, I have to take a step back and think about my motives. Why do I want a new car or a bigger house? Is it really necessary, or am I feeding my ego?

If you're someone who is wealthy, you have a huge chance to do something to change the common perception of rich people, which is that they are greedy and crooked. I know that's a lie and only applies to a very small percentage of the wealthy, but a lot of people believe it. How great would it be to go out and make a large donation to a struggling non-profit that you believe in so that they can help a ton of people? That's something I want to do someday.

Start Small

If you're reading this and have never really given much before and want to start, start small. Find a charity or a worthy cause that you are passionate about and make a small donation. Offer a couple hours of your time to help clean a park or read to children. Every little bit helps. If you belong to a church, maybe your next step is to start tithing or to go on a mission trip. Once you get a taste of it, you may fall in love with the opportunity to help people, and become known as someone who helped change the world for the better.

9

YOUR ACTION PLAN

Well, it's time to make a decision. This is the day that you get to decide if you're going to take the steps outlined in this book to change your future. It could be the best decision you ever make.

Some of the concepts I've discussed may be radically different than what you're used to. That's because change can be scary. There's something even scarier though, and that's mediocrity. If you keep doing what you've been doing, you will continue getting what you've been getting. That's a fact. If you don't like where you are with your finances, or with any part of your life for that matter, change something. Change your habits and then you will see changed results.

It's time to create an action plan for your money. Over the next several pages are some worksheets that you can use to start getting on track. You *CAN* do this if you stick with it. I believe in you!

BUDGETING FORM

Income
Paycheck 1   _____
Paycheck 2   _____

Expenses
Giving   _____
Rent/Mortgage   _____
Utilities   _____
Groceries   _____
Restaurants   _____
Gas   _____
Car Repairs/Replacement   _____
Clothing   _____
Medical   _____
Insurance   _____
Fun Money   _____
Gifts   _____
Debts   _____
Other _____   _____
Other _____   _____

GET-OUT-OF-DEBT PLANNER

List your debts from smallest to largest by balance.

Name of Debt	Minimum Payment	Amount I'm Paying	Payoff Amount

MY SAVINGS PLAN

Reason for Saving	Target Amount	Target Finish Date
Emergency Fund		
Retirement Fund		
Christmas		
Car Replacement		
Vacation		
Home Repair		

MY RETIREMENT PLANNER

What are three things I would like to do in retirement?

1. _____

2. _____

3. _____

What is one thing I can sacrifice now to accelerate my retirement savings?

_____

INSURANCE CHECKLIST

Place a checkmark next to the insurance policies you currently have.

Term Life Insurance　　　　　　　　　_____

Health Insurance　　　　　　　　　　_____

Car Insurance　　　　　　　　　　　_____

Long-Term Disability Insurance　　　_____

Homeowners/Renter's Insurance　　　_____

Long-Term Care Insurance　　　　　_____

Identity Theft Insurance　　　　　　　_____

ABOUT THE AUTHOR

Shane Lundbohm spent most of his adult life "keeping up with the Joneses" by always wanting the latest car or gadget, leading him to go deeply in debt and live paycheck to paycheck. After years of doing this, he decided there must be a better way to live and started educating himself in the world of personal finance as a hobby, which led him to start the blog *Simple Financial Concepts*. Shane's goal is to help others learn how to work through financial difficulty so they can experience the financial freedom that he has found. For more helpful tips about handling money, go to www.simplefinancialconcepts.com.

www.ingramcontent.com/pod-product-compliance
Lightning Source LLC
Chambersburg PA
CBHW052327220526
45472CB00001B/312